Your Best Hustle

A 30 Day Challenge to Empower the Warrior Within

by

ENRIQUE MARIN

A **YOURBESTHUSTLE.COM** PUBLICATION
YOURBESTHUSTLE.COM

Dedication

This book is dedicated to all the servicemen and women past, present, and future and to those who have made the ultimate sacrifice protecting our country. I salute you and am honored to call you family.

Support your Veterans.

To:
ISIS/ISIL (or whatever the fuck you want to be called)
Iran
North Korea
China
Russia
Sudan
Syria
Iraq
Afghanistan
American Flag Burners
Terrorists
And to anyone else who doesn't like America...

FUCK YOU.

Audit Yourself

Who are you really?

I'm not talking about the social media version of yourself but the authentic and genuine you.

We must be willing to look at ourselves and confront everything about who we are. You have to look at the good, the bad and the flaws and imperfections as a whole and be willing to acknowledge what you like and don't like about yourself.

You have to be willing to accept yourself completely and be comfortable with who you are at this very moment.

Auditing yourself and taking inventory of what you're made of is important because chances are the person you think you are is not the person you should know. Like many, you've probably created a false representation of yourself because you felt that's who you needed to be to get to where you are right now.

Social media has somehow made it ok to put yourself out there as something you're not. The funny thing is, many live a life on social media that is nowhere near the truth of their current situation.

You've probably spend way too much time beating yourself up, resenting yourself and sometimes dragging those around you into a world of shit you've unnecessarily created.

You waste so much time trying to cover up your flaws and imperfections in a weak attempt to be perfect. In the end, the only thing you've accomplished is to attract like minded people who are also trying to cover up their flaws and imperfections.

All you're left with is a bunch of inauthentic people and relationships where no one really knows who the fuck they are.

These are different times. The world is craving for something that's been missing for some time now. People in the world are hungry for authenticity. They want to do business and have relationships with people who know who they are and are ok with their own flaws.

Meeting people, whether through social media or in person, requires you to make a connection. Whether it's a first date or a job interview, you're connecting with people who want to get to know the real you. Are you not comfortable with people knowing who you really are? Only you can answer that question in it's truest form.

In order to reach your highest level of acceptance from others, you have to first learn how to accept yourself. Love is the ability to look at another person, see both the good and bad, and still be accepting.

You have to find the real you or you'll always be the same lost version you've created.

Audit yourself to find your authenticity.

The Art of Happiness

Are you happy?

What is happiness and how do you know when you've attained it?

I've asked many people what their goal in life was and a lot of times their answers is to be happy or they want to find happiness.

Unfortunately, people don't know what being happy is all about. They want to be happy but don't know what it is and how to attain it.

What if I told you happiness is a habit that can be learned. Stay with me for a moment...

Let's take a closer look at some habits that will help you become happy:

- Exercising
- Healthy eating
- Smiling more
- Laughing often
- Meditation
- Connecting with people
- Being honest
- Having self-control and
- Being fair

These are just some examples of habits or tendencies to establish and use in different situations. If you practice some of these habits on a daily basis the better you will feel about yourself which in turn, can make you happy.

Look, I'm not saying this shit is easy. I'm just saying that by practicing certain personal habits of self management, like managing moods or being optimistic instead of being pessimistic, it can alter your state of happiness. The only way this will work is if you make certain habits a part of your daily routine.

Happiness is not something you find at the end of a goal you've set up or some destination you have to reach. Happiness is a byproduct of certain behaviors and actions that help change your mindset about the state of being happy.

I'm not trying to get all scientific with this shit. I'm just saying that I believe happiness is a learned skill that people never really learn how to practice. You have to have mental, emotional and physical synergy to have harmonic happiness.

Think of it this way... If you only workout legs but never workout upper body, what happens? You'll look fucking ridiculous! But let's say you have a scheduled workout where all body parts are trained and given an equal amount of attention. Well now you have muscle growth happening all over! That's the harmonic happiness I'm talking about.

You can't expect balanced growth if you're only working on one body part. You have to constantly be working on every aspect of your life that will bring you overall happiness.

People think that money and brand products bring you happiness. I'm the first to agree that money isn't everything but it is something. Having a nice car will give you the satisfaction of showcasing your success to a certain degree and can make you feel good about your accomplishments.

But in the end, having that stuff as a source of happiness is bullshit. If you wreck your awesome car, you become bummed and unhappy. If you lose your job and stop making money, you become unhappy. What I want you to learn or at least become aware of, are the emotional and mindful skills to help you find happiness without counting on other stuff that really don't matter.

In the end, it all come down to mindset. Instead of constantly surrounding yourself with thoughts of shit you don't have, learn how to appreciate and focus on the things you do have. It's about perspective. People waste so much time and money on shit they don't really need in life.

Remember, someone, somewhere will always have it worse. Be grateful and focus on what really counts... your happiness.

Give It Your Best Hustle

You need to learn to believe in yourself and the only way to do that is by being honest and chipping away the bad habits that stop you from revealing the real you.

Ask yourself something… what do you do from 5:00 pm on a Friday to 7:00 am on Monday? What does that time consist of? What did you accomplish during this time? How did you make yourself better? What did you do to make extra money? How did you grow yourself?

You have to act like this is the only life you get and you're playing for keeps. Live like you're not coming back! Whatever you believe is up to you. If you believe you do come back, who's to say you don't come back as a fly, a gnat or a tree?

The truth is, no one really knows. So I choose to live in the now and live like a human being who's been given a chance to play the game of life.

Political Correctness and Safe Places

If you're looking for political correctness or a "safe place" then you're in the wrong fucking community! In this community, no one gives a shit about your gender identity, your political affiliation or how much money is in your bank account.

You're not your fucking designer jeans, the kind of car you drive, or the contents of your wallet. No one gives a shit about how much your watch cost or the types of shoes you wear.

We're here to breed strength, courage, honor, commitment but mostly belief. A belief in yourself so powerful that no situation or person will ever break your inner core.

If you lose the game, don't expect a fucking 10th place ribbon. You need to know how to learn from your shortcomings and move forward to becoming the bad ass you know to be. Gamify your life and you'll understand why everything else is bullshit.

It's time to wake up and play with the big boys!

Table of Contents

Fear and Doubt

Have you ever had a clouded mind filled with thoughts of uncertainty, fear, and second guessing?

Have you spent time trying to make sense of everything that went wrong in your life… the "what if" scenarios playing in your head? But worst of all, have you ever found yourself consumed with regret? I'm talking about the kind of regret that swirls inside your head like a dark cloud covering the brightness of physical and emotional clarity and positivity.

You have to try and understand something… Many people take life for granted. They truly believe they're going to live forever. They believe they'll keep getting those second, third, fourth, even fifth chances to make things happen.

Well, I'm sorry to be the one to tear down the cardboard castle you've built, but your chance to hit a homerun and start winning the game of life is NOW!

So, what will you do? Will you play the game?

Will you risk taking a swing?

Or would you rather watch the game from the bench?

Whatever you decide to do just remember, you're in the game and you have to make a choice.

A Wake Up Call

I used to lead a life of misery. Always in the wrong relationships, drinking heavily, getting fat, binge watching shows on Netflix, being lazy, and surfing the internet to watch pornography. I disliked everything and everyone. But mostly, I hated the fucking guy staring back at me in the mirror.

I used to dress like shit, have no pride in my hygiene or personal appearance and I never committed to anything that required... well, commitment.

Everyone I knew couldn't stand me. I was good at pissing people off, especially those that really cared about me. I woke up one day in some alley, drunk off my ass... with police officers looking over me.

I can still remember them looking at me. It was a look of disgust and shame. I can still feel that burning look of pity and sadness. That's when I met "rock bottom".

I finally realized that the only one that one going to truly give a shit about me... was me.

After years of working on getting my shit together, I learned to confront hardships head on and not give a shit about what others thought of me. I no longer had the fear of rejection and learned that making excuses is for the weak.

Through my many failures, I figured out that failure is a good thing, but only if you learn from it.

You are your own brand. You are constantly selling yourself to the world. You have to be hungry for success. That shit isn't going to be handed out to like some 5th place trophy. It takes hard work and the ethical hustle of man determined to put food on the table and provide for his family.

No one wants to hear your excuses or reasons why you can't do something. Figure it out! Get the fuck up and figure that shit out! Prove everyone wrong. Prove to yourself you can do anything because, in the end, that's what fucking matters.

If you don't wake up right now, you'll never be the person you want to be...

And it's no one's fault but your own.

What's Your Self Worth?

You can waste your life thinking about how it wasn't fair, how life did you wrong, how you grew up without privilege or opportunity. Even those who grow up with privilege and opportunity fuck it up and throw it all away. Use your past as a catalyst to help you grow and succeed. Remember the shitty times and vow never to put you or your loved ones in those situations... ever.

It doesn't matter how you grew up or how it used to be... It only matters how it is right now.

You have the power to control that.

You have to learn how to have thick skin. You will never make it if you don't. This life is tough and it will beat the hell out of you if you let it. This goes for those around you as well. Negativity thrives on negativity. If you surround yourself with people who always complain about how life fucked them over or their parents didn't give them a better life... well, you'll believe the same crap as well.

Everyone has to learn to play their own game. They have to learn their own advantages and disadvantages. Everyone has different strengths and weaknesses.

Don't believe what others have to say. When they criticize your game, that's when you know the shit you're doing is working. People will notice the change. They will notice something different about you... and they won't like it.

Why? Because change is unknown territory and that's when fear sets in.

You have to keep pushing... You have to EXECUTE, EXECUTE, EXECUTE!

Get in the habit of putting things in motion. Making success happen for you! If you don't, I promise you this... no one will do it for you.

Having Self Awareness

You have to learn how to be self-aware and be honest about it. You can't learn self-awareness and have fear doing it. It just won't work.

Many people lie to themselves. Not everyone is meant to play the game. Self-awareness isn't just about knowing your strengths but it's also understanding your shortcomings. You can't play the game of life wearing someone else's jersey. Learn to wear your own jersey proudly and let everyone know you're rooting for team "YOU!"

You have to follow and trust in yourself and create a strategy to win. Don't be afraid to audit who you are. It's the first step you have to take for anything else to work.

Failure Does Not Exist

How do you decide when to quit on something? When it's time to pull back? How do you decide when it's just not working out?

Understand that nobody gives a fuck about your success or failures and that's the way it should be. You have YOU to worry about... That's the game.

If you have never gotten the shit beat out of you when trying to succeed, you're doing it wrong. If you've never truly failed, then you've never truly tried. How can you grow and realize your true potential when every move you make scares you into doing nothing?

If you have ambition, your actions have to match it. You can't expect change or a different outcome doing the same fucking thing all the time. If you need to make money, you have to set a goal and take action.

Groups of people sit around tables all the time and talk about all the great ideas they have to get rich, travel, succeed and whatever else they want to accomplish. And at the end of that conversation… that's where it stays.

No action is ever taken to make any of those ideas happen. Instead of just talking about it, you have to want to be about it. The only way to do that is by taking action.

Keep this in mind…

Failure isn't always the best teacher. You have to understand that failure can be a good tool to learn from your mistakes but if the failure is so hard that you can't get back up, that's not the lesson you want to experience and learn from.

But I would rather have you experience that than never try at all.

Building Your own Brand
(This Means You)

You have to constantly be working on content and building your own brand. You have to start documenting your life instead of just creating it. Do you know your talents? If not, you need to find those talents and make them work for you.

To find those talents, you have to understand one thing... YOU have to understand YOU!

You have to build your own call to action. You have to find your own answers to happiness. I'm telling you right now. It's not money. Money will not buy happiness. Money comes and goes. Money makes you feel like you're on top of the world one day and when you lose it all, you'll feel worse than being truly alone in the middle of a concrete prison cell. Trust me.

You have to learn to be patient and how to listen to yourself. You have to find your zen, you have to find your drive but before all of that... you have to find yourself.

Finding the Type of Education That's Right for You

By no means am I saying that getting a degree is a bad thing. Education is an important part of being successful. What I'm trying to say is be careful where you get your education so you don't waste time.

Let's say you want to be an automotive mechanic. You're better off going to some trade school than a 4-year college. Before you get into all sorts of debt, think about what your interests and hobbies are and learn everything you can before committing to a higher learning institute.

What am I talking about? Research! Google and Youtube have become prime examples of finding out everything you need with just about anything out there. Network and ask people who are earning a living in a certain industry you're interested in and let them tell you their experiences before committing yourself.

Reading has helped many successful entrepreneurs. I honestly don't know if that's a common trait among them. I personally read books to grow myself and those around me. I also focus on books because it helps me disengage from technology.

Not everyone can be an entrepreneur and that's ok. Truth be told, if it was an easy path, everyone would do it and make a living out of it.

My point is that you don't need a degree from some Ivy League school to tell you how smart you are. What you need is drive. You need to be hungry for success in whatever it is you're trying to achieve.

Believe you are smart enough to do anything you want. Just understand that it takes hustle to make it happen. That's all up to you.

There's No Such Thing As An Overnight Success

Even the most talented people put in hard work to get to where they are. In the game of life, there is no such thing as being lucky. It takes the hard work of being disciplined and committed to making things happen. Some people have honed in on their skills and talents faster than others. Find your talents, work hard and transform.

Michael Jordan, in my opinion, is the greatest basketball player of all time. He paved the way for others basketball greats to be successful in the game. Michael Jordan has talent.

What people don't know is that he learned to hone in on his talents. By no means did it come easy. What many don't recognize or understand is how he became the best. They don't go behind the scenes where he devoted thousands of hours to perfect his game. That's his hustle. That's the unknown and unseen variable by many.

You have to learn to play your game, perfect your skills and learn to profit from it. But first, you have to learn who you are and what your talents are.

Make the Best of Your Time

There is no reason you have to do shit you hate. While you're playing on your phone, hanging out with your buddies at the bar, or reaching that level 47 on some fucking Playstation game... others are putting in work.

You need to make the time to put in the work. You have to learn time management and understand that you can fuck off later in life but right now, you should concentrate on learning and being fearless about making mistakes. Learn from your experiences and be honest about where it went wrong. The point is not to give up and learn how to redirect your point of execution from different angles. You have to learn how to pivot.

If you're spending an extra hour or two on shit that isn't making you money or helping you grow then you're just wasting valuable time.

Find what you love, figure out your talents and work on them. Monetization comes after that.

I just want you to know that it's ok to wing it or shoot from the hip. Just keep pushing forward. You will never fail yourself if you keep pushing and continue to work on yourself.

And remember, procrastination is the mother of all failures because you miss every single shot you don't take.

Why This 30 Day Challenge?

I believe you can kick some serious ass this year. I know that if you wake up and apply your talents to playing the game of life, you'll fucking win BIG!

First thing's first...

You need to find clarity and focus within yourself. After that, you need to start fucking suffocating negativity and excuses, but most importantly... the fear of failure.

You need to make this the year you stopped giving a shit about what people think of you. You need to be selfish and think of your success and your wins in this game of life.

Take the 30 Day Challenge and become the man you know to be.

Here are the 13 Habits you will commit to changing for the next 30 Days:

Your 30 Day Challenge:
- *It Starts from Within*
- The Hustle Starts Early in the Morning
- Start Believing In Yourself
- Why You Need to Stop with the Internet Pornography and Masturbation
- How to Physically and Mentally Kick-Start Your Body
- Why You Should Always Be Well Groomed and Dressed
- Why Don't You Just Read a Fucking Book Already!
- How to Budget and Save Some Money When You're Broke
- How to Beat Your Technology Addiction
- Meditation is Not Just for Hippies

It Starts From Within

For the next 30 days, you will stay away from that shitty food you've been used to consuming on a regular basis. There are many ways to lose weight but if you think crash diets and starving yourself is going to work… think again.

You have to feed the machine… And you can't continue consuming that shitty fuel either. You have to be disciplined enough to stay away from the foods that hurt everything you're trying to accomplish. Stay away from the following types of foods:

- Sugars
- Alcohol
- Processed Foods
- Carbohydrates (sort of)

<u>Sugars</u> - This stuff will make an addict out of you! You need to get this out of your system as soon as possible. I'm not saying sugar is bad for you in really low quantities but stuff like high fructose corn syrup, which is practically in everything, can lead to weight gain, obesity, and diabetes. You have to stay disciplined to stop eating sugar. The first week is the toughest. After that, just looking at sugar will make you feel sick.

<u>Alcohol</u> - I feel like I'm Benedict Arnold (if you don't know who this is, read a fucking book!) by saying this but consuming alcoholic beverages and abusing it will get you fat. Look, I love bullshitting with friends and tossing back some cold ones but it takes commitment and discipline to stay away. This one, without a doubt... sucks.

Processed Foods - Unfortunately, the way food is processed isn't the best for the body. Food companies have no problem filling pre-packaged foods with so much unhealthy shit. This isn't a push to buy organic or become some hippy vegan. It's a call to action to eat cooked foods for the next 30 days and stay the hell away from these types of foods. You'll notice the difference, trust me.

Carbohydrates - This is a tough one. We need carbohydrates to get energy. The thing is, you want to eat certain types of carbohydrates at certain times. Cutting out carbohydrates completely isn't always the best choice. Look, I'm not a fucking nutritionist and I'm not going to bull-shit you. There are so many different studies and shit talking about carbs that after all of it, you have to learn what's good for you, what times to eat carbs and how much to consume.

Everyone's body is different. This is part of learning what works for you.

Simplicity is key. The focus is on these four types of foods. If you can be disciplined to stay away from them for the next 30 days, you'll lose weight and feel much better.

Get ready to lose some weight!

The Hustle Starts Early in the Morning

Why in the world would anyone want to get up so early? The real question is, why the fuck NOT! How many times have you told yourself you don't have enough time? You have so much on your plate and you just can't seem to find time during your busy day to get it done.

While the rest of the world is fast asleep dreaming of a life they want to live, you will be wide awake hustling to make shit happen. You have to Get Up, Defeat, and Repeat your day!

When you wake up early, you give yourself some "me" time. I wake up at 4:00 A.M. every day to study online marketing strategies and get a workout in. By 8:00 A.M., I'm ready to move forward with my day and start on my regular tasks. After work, I would give myself some more "me" time and focus on creating content and strategies I can implement to make money or improve my talents.

The point I'm trying to make is that you have to make the time to work on yourself and your hustle. What is the one thing you've been wanting to do but can't seem to find the time to do it? Well, instead of watching shows on Netflix or playing video games, learn to make the best of your time and invest in you.

There are several ways you can make this work. The 30 day challenge is to wake up at 5:30 A.M. and start kicking ass. You can decide how much time you need to Get Shit Done.

When you wake up early, you'll have more "me" time and you'll have the opportunity to work on whatever it is that will make you build your brand.

There is a method of slowing working backward to getting up early and build the habit. Start by waking up 15 to 30 minutes early every morning until you reach your 5:30 A.M. goal.

Get Up, Defeat, Repeat every single day and stop making excuses of not having enough time... You have to MAKE time!

Start Believing In Yourself

How do you expect the world to believe in you if you don't believe in yourself? Enough is enough! Nothing matters more than being a strong believer in yourself. You have to get to a point in your life where you become your own life coach. You have to audit yourself and understand that this is your life and you can live it any way you want.

Trying to live through someone else is not living. That's pretending to be someone you're not.

That's the goal of this 30 day challenge.

I want you to look in the mirror and say something positive about yourself at least 20 times in the morning! Yes, that's correct. At least 20 times. You see, you have to start somewhere. You have to believe you're the author of your own story and that you really do exist. You're not in this world as some fictional character in someone else's story. This is your fucking story and you get to narrate what happens!

You're going to learn that no one is going to be better at telling you how to live a happy life except yourself. You can say something short but it must be something you believe. For example, "I'm gonna crush it today", "You've got this!", "Today I'm going to get shit done!" and so one.

You have to believe in your words both mentally and emotionally. Believe in what you're doing and what you can accomplish. Believe you can fucking do this!

Learn to trust that inner voice and listen to what YOU have to say!

Why You Need to Stop with the Internet Pornography and Masturbation

Let's just dive in on this… Porn is ruining your inner drive in more ways than you know! By no means am I saying there's anything wrong with sex, but many people spend way too much time watching porn and it' taking away from being productive.

How many times have you found yourself thinking about sex throughout the day? When you're sifting through porn sites, how much time do you waste trying to find that perfect scene? How much money do you spend on porn subscriptions? Is it something you do in secret from a spouse or girlfriend? Remember, you can lie to everyone else but you can't lie to yourself.

Women are smart, beautiful and have a way of mesmerizing the opposite sex. They are also considered to be the most fiendish instrument ever created to bedazzle the days of men!

For 30 days there will be no masturbation, internet pornography, dating sites or apps. You have to learn how to master your sexual wants and needs in order to make better decisions and not be clouded by temptation.

There's a time and place for everything. Learning how to control yourself will lead to better decision making, having more energy, strengthening relationships with the opposite sex, and save money. If you believe masturbation and internet pornography isn't an issue, do some research and see what's happening in other countries like Japan.

The goal isn't to shame internet pornography or masturbation... it's to help you learn how to be disciplined and master unproductive habits.

It's important to learn how to make decisions using your mind and not your penis. When you can separate the two and make better decisions, you'll be saving yourself a lot grief, money and heartache.

How to Physically and Mentally Kick-Start Your Body

Sometimes the whole working out thing isn't as easy to start. You make plenty of excuses why you can't make it to the gym but mostly it's just plain old laziness. There's no end goal or reason to start working out. It's even easier to get into this rut if you're already in a relationship or married.

Well… time to man up and get this shit going! If you need a reason to work out, do it for your family, for your health, and for your own personal pride. Working out makes you feel good about yourself. Scientifically, you feel much better, it grows muscle and strength and it helps convey that you actually give a shit about yourself.

For the next 30 days, you're going to start a simple workout. There are no weights needed and you can do it anywhere. Start off slow and increase the reps weekly. Here are the five body exercises you can start with:

2-minute Intervals with 1-minute rest for 3-5 sets.

- 10 Pushups
- 20 Air Squats
- 20 Jumping Jacks
- 20 Sit ups
- 20 Mountain Climbers

Find a mobile app or a timer to keep track. You may want to take a quick test by testing each exercise for one minute each and then figure out how many sets you can start out with. If you haven't worked out in a while, please be cautious when exercising.

By no means am I saying I'm a fitness guru or some licensed fitness instructor. I'm just saying you have to start somewhere and start working on sculpting your body. That shit isn't going to happen on its own.

If you don't want to do start with this, that's ok. Just do something for the next 30 days and commit. You have to start taking care of yourself. Eating healthy and starting a workout regiment takes discipline and commitment. So, let' get this shit done!

If you're already into fitness and do it on a regular basis, good for you! Keep up the good work and take it to the next level.

To get the wanted results, you need to put in work! Hustle, hustle, hustle!

Bonus:

Before you begin, get someone to take photos of you from all angles. Get your ass in gear and start your workouts. After those 30 days, take some more photos and you'll be amazed at what you've achieved. Just remember, you have to stick to the damn game plan!

Why You Should Always Be Well Groomed and Dressed

Making first impressions is always important. How many times have you left the house to run a quick errand or go grab some food and randomly bump into people you know? Maybe you see a cute girl but talking to her is out of the question because you look like you just finished dumpster diving in the back alley.

For the next 30 days, you will make a point to be well groomed and dressed EVERYDAY! Look, I'm not saying you have to wear your "Sunday's Best" on a daily basis but you will do your best to appear presentable and ready for any social situation.

This way, you won't have to worry about who you meet or who you run into because you'll be looking your best that day.

I'm not talking about going out and buying new clothes to do this either. You'll be losing weight so wait until after you finish your 30 day challenge to purchase new clothes. What I'm talking about is being dressed and groomed for any occasion.

For example, let's say you have to go to the grocery store. You should make every attempt to be well groomed and dressed. Take some pride in yourself and look your best.

Branding yourself is very important. If you want to be taken seriously, have to act and dress the part as well. No more wearing gym shoes to go out in or wear t-shirts out to nice restaurants. It's time to change things up and personal appearance is a really great start.

So, let's make it happen! And remember, the only person you have to impress is yourself. Stay focused, committed and disciplined. You can do this!

Why Don't You Just Read a Fucking Book Already!

I don't think I have to stress the importance of constant growth. Education is the key to success. When was the last time (if ever) you read a book? I'm talking about some serious reading. The kind of stuff that makes you think and question everything around you.

For the next 30 days, you will read a book that helps you grow mentally and emotionally.

Oh C'mon! It's one book in 30 days! Choose something that you've always wanted to read or perhaps something that'll help you out in school or maybe something inspiring. Every successful entrepreneur that I know makes time to read. Even if it's only for 30 minutes a day.

The only way you're going to grow is to educate yourself. Surfing the internet and watching videos isn't going to completely do that. Besides, picking up a book allows for the opportunity to disengage from technology and focus on something more real and simplistic.

Just remember, the most influential people in the world have one thing in common, they read a lot of books! I know you can do it!

How to Budget and Save Some Money When You're Broke

For some, saving money can be a daunting task, especially if you don't have anything left over after paying bills. Sometimes you have downgrade your life to gradually upgrade. You have to acknowledge the dumb shit you're spending your money on and figure out what's important and what's not.

For the next 30 days, I want you to keep tabs on what you spend. Categorize it by bills, food, and luxuries. Why? Well, I want you to take notice of what you're really spending your money on and why you're always broke.

I mean, what's really important? Paying your phone bill or going out drinking with your buddies and picking up women? I know what sounds more fun but what's really going to put you ahead of the game?

Also, I want you to start thinking about what you can do to earn money. This is where the "low gear is better than no gear" mindset applies. Let's say you want to check out Ibiza, Spain because you heard the women there were beautiful and really fun. You would like to go but you don't know how you'll ever save money to get there.

One way you can do this is by taking inventory of all of the useless shit you've accumulated over the years that's just taking up space. Create an account on Craigslist, Ebay or Amazon and learn how to make it work for you. Sell that crap and make some money. By the time you know it, you'll have enough money to make it to Ibiza, Spain.

But if you're smart, instead of actually going on your trip right away, you'll take that money and invest it on something else that will make you more money. Then you can go on that trip free of financial burdens. Be smart about your hustle and don't be so quick to throw it all away.

Look, saving money is not rocket science. It just takes some commitment and discipline. I really believe you can do this.

How to Beat Your Technology Addiction

Technological advances have really changed the way humans communicate and see the world. We rely on technology for just about everything in our daily lives, affecting us both good and bad. We have to remind ourselves that we're on this earth to live and communicate with nature and other human beings. Technology has been a wonderful tool in this day and age but it's also hindered human interaction.

For the next 30 days, I want you to disengage from all technology when eating. Yes, that's right… don't bring that fucking phone to the dinner table! I don't care what you do with it, to be honest. You just can't have it out when you eat. Place it on silent and in your pocket. It doesn't come out until you have finished eating.

Try This...

Play games with your friends and place all phone devices on the table. The first one to reach in and grab it pays the tab. We're becoming so fucking programmed to look at our phones that we forget there's a whole world around us. It's slowly getting away from you.

If you have the opportunity to engage with other human beings in a social setting, I want you to put your phone away and interact rather than looking on Facebook, Instagram or texting someone who isn't around. You're a human being, for crying out loud! Interact like one!

AND

For the next 30 days, you will NOT text and drive! Concentrate on driving and don't be the idiot that causes a car accident because you couldn't wait to text someone back.

People have died not paying attention because they're looking down at a fucking phone screen! Don't be one of those people. Be disciplined enough to connect with a hands free phone device or don't do it at all.

There are more methods of breaking the technological addiction. Do yourself a favor... take a break from technology and learn to be human again.

Meditation is Not Just for Hippies

Whenever I throw out words like "meditation" and "relaxation" some of my friends give me this eye rolling look and accuse me of becoming a hippie or flowerchild. Meditation and having inner peace is vital to inner growth as a person and will help bring focus back into your day.

Well, listen up you fucking pansies!

For the next 30 days, whenever you feel tired or stressed, I want you to listen to your body and meditate for at least 20 minutes to regain focus and much needed energy. Find a quiet spot, sit or lie down, close your eyes and focus on your breathing. It takes practice but I promise you'll feel like a completely re-energized badass!

Ok, let me explain… Meditation has worked wonders for me and has given me the opportunity to tone down stress while bringing focus and energy back into my day. Waking up at 4:00 A.M. daily can take a toll on you after about 9 hours of kicking some serious ass.

So, when I feel tired, I stop what I'm doing and I meditate. I find my happy place and concentrate on my breathing. I do this for about 20 minutes. It's like taking a much needed power nap that allows you to continue to kick ass for another 9 hours!

This didn't happen overnight. It took me a while to really understand meditation and practice different methods. In the beginning, I was just like you. I thought it was a bunch of bullshit and just something that yoga fanatics and hippies do to have an excuse to take a fucking nap. I couldn't be more wrong. Those fuckers had it right! I've been missing out this whole time!

Don't judge the shit without trying it. I wouldn't be staking my word or reputation on it if I thought it was horse shit.

Don't be afraid to try something different. This is one of the best things you can learn to do for your mind and body. Get It Done!

Create and Finish a Daily "To Do" List

Procrastination is the mother of all self-inflicted hurdles. Why? Because it's something you can control and for whatever reason, you choose not to do it. It's easy to make excuses as to why you won't get that book started or why you won't start going to back to school.

The truth is, everyone thinks they have all the time in the world. You keep waiting for that "perfect" moment when life is aligned with the stars to finally get started. Wake the fuck up! The moment is NOW.

For the next 30 days, you will make a daily list of something you know has to get done and make it a priority. You will learn how to shake the word "procrastination" from your limited vocabulary and flush it out of that so called "hard body" of yours.

Daily execution is the key to success. You can't just talk about doing something, you have to be about execution. No one is going to do it for you and you are definitely running out of time.

Remember, regret is a motherfucker. You don't want to be the father or grandfather feeding bullshit about success to your loved ones if you have never done it yourself. #GETSHITDONE

Give Someone a Compliment Daily

Life is about connecting with people. Care, compassion, and tolerance are needed more today than ever before. Let's be real. There are some really shitty people in the world but we're not going to contribute to that problem.

For the next 30 days, you will give a random stranger a true compliment. Let them know how much you appreciate them or tell them how great their smile is. Practice the art of giving thanks and let people know there is still hope for humanity.

There's enough negativity in this world and changing how you think and feel about people will only help you grow. Look, I'm not saying kiss someone's ass or take people's shit. All I'm saying is compliment people and mean it. If they don't respond with kindness, well... at least you tried to make the world a little better in that moment.

To change the world for the better, you have to change your reality. You have to change your outlook on humanity. Going out there and treating people with respect and dignity will help encourage more people to do the same.

Go have some fun with this one! I promise you'll brighten someone's day.

Daily Gratitude

Life is not about accumulating wealth, property or all of that crap you currently store in your garage or high priced storage unit. There's a lot to be grateful for. If you're reading this, it's a perfect example of being grateful for being alive, having sight and being blessed with the opportunity to educate yourself a little more.

For the next 30 days, you will set aside time to be grateful for having another day of life and being able to tell you those around you how much you love and appreciate them. Give thanks and appreciation to those who help you and consider you family and friend.

This isn't something religious or spiritual (although it can be). I just want you to acknowledge how precious life is and appreciate the gifts and talents you have. Don't waste this precious time. Give thanks.

"Your Best Hustle" Community

If you're joining this community with fear, doubt and lack of commitment… get the fuck out right now. This is not a support group. This is an ass-kicking group of men who will drive a transformation within you that your own parents won't recognize after 30 days.

Join this community and let's kick some ass together. I can promise you this, you'll learn more about yourself in 30 days than ever before. You will have a wide variety of members with different life views working together to bring out the best in you.

This community will pound into you and push beyond limits, the character traits you need to be confident and successful in every aspect of your life.

We will work together 24/7 to make each other the best versions of ourselves we can possibly be.

We need to work on your goals and ambitions. Individually and as a community. Our goal is to pull you in opposite directions and make you feel comfortable with being uncomfortable.

We need to chip away everyday, the setbacks in your life and transform you into a successful gentleman. A man filled with confidence, truth, and self-worth that goes beyond anything you've ever known.

The end goal is to make you understand that you don't need me. You don't need mastermind gurus or life coaches to tell you how to succeed in life.

I'll teach you how to become your own life coach and make your own success.

Conclusion

Do you know why most fail at success? Because many are programmed to need constant approval, validation and have a fear of failure.

You need to learn that the only approval that counts is your own.

Don't worry about fancy cars and how much money you have in the bank. Instead, worry about how many people will come to your funeral.

Your Best Hustle is about individual empowerment. It's about believing in yourself and proving it.

Let's get this shit done and give it your best hustle.

www.ingramcontent.com/pod-product-compliance
Lightning Source LLC
Chambersburg PA
CBHW030304030426
42337CB00012B/584